EGMONT

We bring stories to life

First published in Great Britain in 2019 by
Egmont Books

An imprint of HarperCollins*Publishers*
1 London Bridge Street
London SE1 9GF

www.egmontbooks.co.uk

Written by Dan Morgan
Edited by Stephanie Milton
Designed by Andrea Philpots, John Stuckey and Richie Hull
Illustrations by Joe McLaren
Special thanks to Alex Wiltshire, Jennifer Hammervald, Filip Thoms,
Amanda Ström and Isabella Balk.

▣MOJANG

ISBN 978 1 4052 9525 3

70614/011
Printed in UK

ONLINE SAFETY FOR YOUNGER FANS

Spending time online is great fun! Here are a few simple rules to help younger fans
stay safe and keep the internet a great place to spend time:

-Never give out your real name – don't use it as your username.
-Never give out any of your personal details.
-Never tell anybody which school you go to or how old you are.
-Never tell anybody your password except a parent or a guardian.
-Be aware that you must be 13 or over to create an account on many sites. Always check
the site policy and ask a parent or guardian for permission before registering.
-Always tell a parent or guardian if something is worrying you.

Stay safe online. Any website addresses listed in this book are correct at the time
of going to print. However, Egmont is not responsible for content hosted by third parties.
Please be aware that online content can be subject to change and websites can contain
content that is unsuitable for children. We advise that all children are supervised
when using the internet.

Egmont takes its responsibility to the planet and its inhabitants very seriously. We aim to
use papers from well-managed forests run by responsible suppliers.

IN THE BEGINNING ...

As always, we begin in the Overworld.
Get ready to giggle!

Q *How do trees get on the internet?*

A *They log on.*

Q *Did you hear about the mountains that told jokes?*

A *They were 'hill areas'.*

Do you like the lakes in the Overworld?

5

ZOMBIE ZINGERS

Try not to laugh your head off reading these gruesome gags.

Q Why do zombies sleep all the time?

A Because they're dead tired.

Q How do you stop a zombie from attacking?

A You block its path.

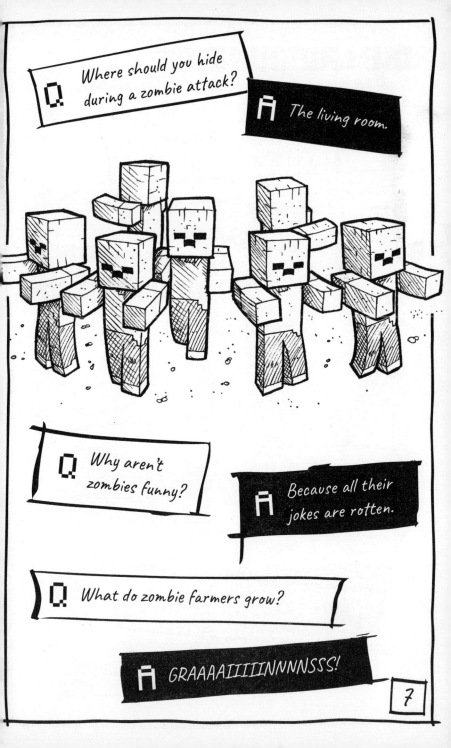

Q Where should you hide during a zombie attack?

A The living room.

Q Why aren't zombies funny?

A Because all their jokes are rotten.

Q What do zombie farmers grow?

A GRAAAAIIIIINNNNSSS!

7

DIE LAUGHING

Don't laugh so much you have to respawn!

Q Did you hear about the zombie that was brilliant at attacks?

A He was very dead-icated.

Q What did the zombie say when it met Steve?

A Pleased to eat you.

Q What was the baby zombie's favourite toy?

A Their dead-y bear.

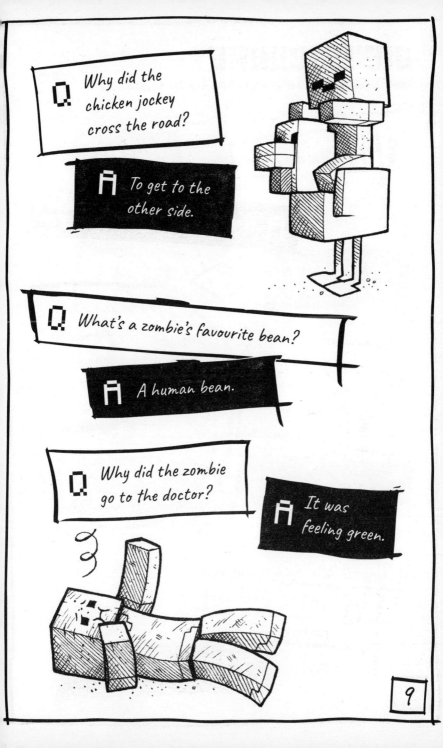

9

JOKE JOURNEY

Let's hope these puns don't go south!

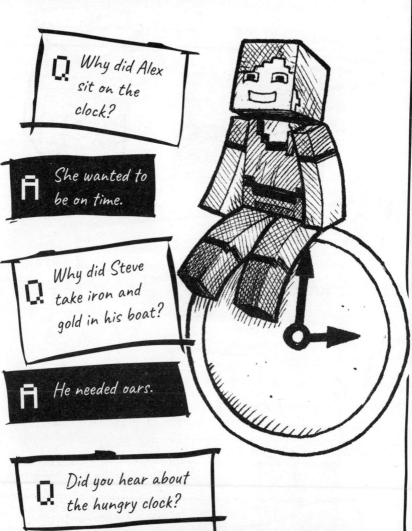

Q Why did Alex sit on the clock?

A She wanted to be on time.

Q Why did Steve take iron and gold in his boat?

A He needed oars.

Q Did you hear about the hungry clock?

A It went back four seconds.

Alex: OK, I've found north, south and east on the compass.

Steve: Where's the west of it?

Steve: I was going to tell a compass joke but I've lost my bearings.

Alex: I wrote a joke about a broken compass but I'm not sure where I'm going with it.

11

RIDICULOUS REDSTONE

A hearty chuckle is just a stone's throw away.

Q What is redstone ore used for?

A Rowing a redstone boat.

Steve: I'd tell you the joke about the redstone circuit, but I'd just be repeating myself.

Q What did Steve say to the sad redstone lamp?

A Lighten up!

Q Why does Alex love redstone lamps?

A Because they light up her life.

Q Why don't llamas like redstone dust up their nose?

A Well, would you like it?

PLEASED TO EAT YOU

Sink your teeth into these meaty morsels.

Q How do you know when your mutton has gone off?

A It tastes baaaaad!

Q What do sheep wear to keep their hooves warm in winter?

A Woolly muttons.

Q What's a pig's favourite karate move?

A A pork chop.

Q What did Alex say when she saw the cows on top of the mountain?

A The steaks have never been higher.

Steve: Did I sleep through dinner?

Alex: Yes, big 'missed steak'.

HORSING AROUND

We think mule find these jokes a-NEIGH-zing!

Q Where do you take a sick horse?

A To the horse-pital.

Q What do you call a donkey with 3 legs?

A A wonky.

Q What do you call a donkey with 4 legs?

A Stable.

Q Did you hear about the mule who had a sore throat?

A She was a little hoarse.

Q Did you hear about the mule that lived next to the horse?

A They were neigh-bours.

Q What kind of horse do you ride at night?

A A night-mare.

JOB JOKES

Who says having a job can't be fun?

Q Why did the cow jump over the moon?

A Steve had cold hands when he was milking it.

Q What do librarians wear on their feet?

A Shhhhhhoes.

Q Why are blacksmiths so interesting?

A They're always riveting.

Q Why are blacksmiths ahead of their time?

A They were shaping metal before it was cool.

Q What do you call someone who steals from the butcher?

A A hamburglar.

TICKLE YOUR FUNNY BONE

These skeleton jokes will hit you in the right spot.

Q Did you hear about the skeleton who used his bow and arrow at night?

A He didn't know what he was missing.

Q What do you call a skeleton who can't be bothered to attack?

A Lazy bones.

Q What do you call a skeleton who stays in the snowy tundra too long?

A A numbskull.

Q Did you hear about the skeleton who broke another skeleton's bow and arrow?

A Now they're arch(er) enemies.

Q Why are skeletons good at telling jokes?

A Because they're so humerus.

GRUESOME GAGS

More jokes to really make you scream with laughter!

Q Why do skeletons hate being high up in the mountains?

A The cold goes right through them.

Q What's a skeleton's favourite meal?

A Spare ribs.

FISHY FUNNIES

This is dolphin-ately the plaice for some fin-tastic fish jokes.

Q What party game do fish play?

A Salmon Says.

Q What do you call a fish with no eyes?

A A fsh.

Alex: Do dolphins do things by accident?

Steve: No, it's on porpoise.

Q What kind of photos do turtles take?

A Shellfies.

Q What do you do on a turtle's birthday?

A Shellebrate!

Two fish were swimming when it started raining. One said to the other, 'Quick, get under the bridge. We're going to get wet!'

A TOOLBOX OF TITTERS

Don't be a spanner – let yourself be tickled by these tool jokes.

Q: Did you hear that Alex got hit by a pickaxe?

A: Don't worry, she only suffered miner injuries.

Alex: I've invented the shovel.

Steve: Sounds ground-breaking.

Q What do you call a man with a shovel?

A Doug.

Q So what do you call him when he's lost it?

A Douglas.

Q Did you hear about the artist who could make anything using shears?

A She was a shear genius.

Q What happened when the lumberjack hit the creeper?

A It axe-ploded.

THESE JOKES ROCK!

Put yourself between a rock and a funny place.

Q What did Alex say to the diamond ore?

A I dig you.

Q What did the diamond say to the coal?

A I've been under a lot of pressure recently.

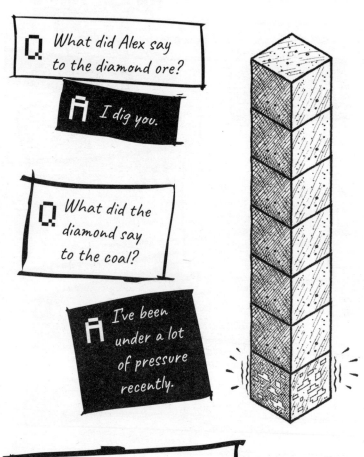

Q What music do ore blocks listen to?

A Rock music.

Q: Did you hear about the mining accident?

A: It was ore-ful.

Steve: Did you hear about the villager that hated coal?

Alex: No.

Steve: Never mined.

Alex: What's your favourite ore? Emerald or lapis lazuli?

Steve: Either ore.

ORE-SOME JOKES

Have a giggle at these gems.

> **Q** What do diamond ore and raw steak have in common?

> **A** They're both rare.

> **Q** What do you see when you look underneath some ore?

> **A** Rock bottom.

Q How do emeralds exercise?

 A Gemnastics.

Q Why did the Nether quartz ore quit?

 A Everyone took it for granite.

Q How did Alex get extra ore?

 A With good fortune.

ORE-FULLY FUNNY

Roar along with these ore-fully good jokes.

Q What did the ore block say to the miner?

A Pick me!

Q Why is redstone messy?

A Because of all the dust.

Q When were redstone jokes the funniest?

A During the stone age.

Q What do gold ore and farts have in common?

A They both smelt.

Q Why are iron ingot-makers always accused of farting?

A Because whoever smelt it dealt it.

33

WATER LOTTA LAUGHS

Cry tears of laughter as you read these witty, watery wisecracks.

Q What should you collect icy water in?

A A cold-ron.

Q Why did the fish blush?

A Because it saw the ocean's bottom.

Q Where do drowned like to swim?

A The Dead Sea.

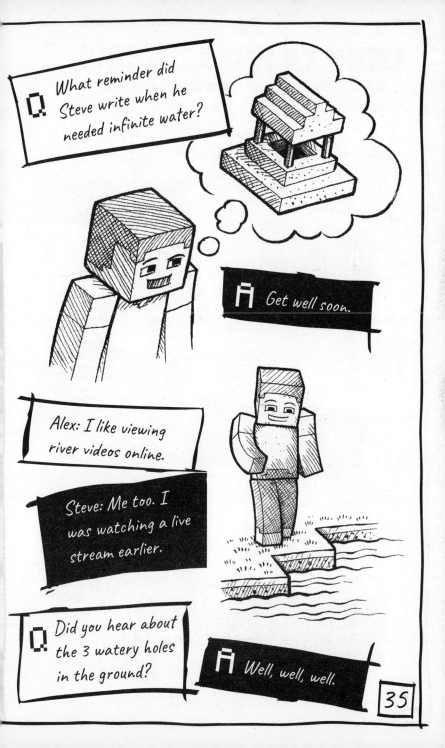

CROP TO IT!

Plant a smile on your face and let these jokes grow on you.

Q Did you hear about the chicken that ate all the seeds?

A It still felt peck-ish.

Q Why did the chicken stay at home?

A Because it felt fowl.

Q How do you fix a pumpkin?

A With a pumpkin patch.

Q Did you hear about the poorly carrot?

A It wasn't peeling very well.

Q What do you call it when a pig rolls over a potato?

A Mashed pork-tato.

Q Why won't crops grow in the Nether?

A Because they wither away.

MINE MANIA

You'll need to dig deep for these belly laughs.

Q Why couldn't Steve get to the emerald ore?

A Something was blocking his way.

Q Where do tired miners sleep?

A On bedrock.

39

EXPLOSIVE LAUGHS

These jokes will really creep up on you!

Q What is a creeper's favourite subject at school?

A Hissssssstory!

Q Did you hear about the creeper's birthday party?

A It really went off with a BANG!

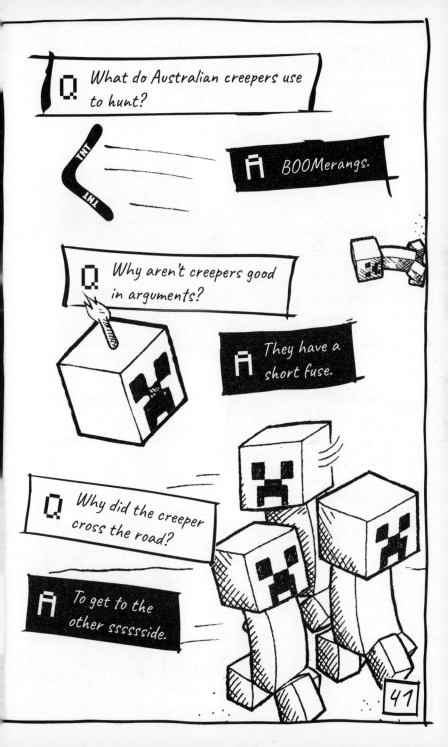

BOOM BOOM!

Get ready to explode with laughter!

Q Why are creepers prone to jealousy?

A Because they're green with envy.

Q What happened when Alex noticed the creeper was following her?

A It blew its opportunity.

Q What do creepers play their music on?

A A BOOMbox.

Q Why do creepers love going to parties?

A Because they always have a blast.

Q Why was the creeper excited when it got hit by lightning?

A It was all charged up.

INTO THE NETHER

Get ready for some fiery fun!

Q *Did you hear about the skeleton that found romance in the Nether?*

A *He fell head over heels in lava.*

Steve: I'm struggling to think of a lava joke.

Alex: You should just let it flow.

Q *What did Alex say after she escaped the Nether?*

A *Nether again.*

Q What did Alex say when she returned to the Nether?

A Never say Nether.

Q What do you call it when you get sand on your shoe in the Nether?

A Sole sand.

Q How did Steve feel when he saw his Nether portal had been destroyed?

A A-ghast.

NETHER AGAIN

Spending time in the Nether is a real scream!

Q Why can't you get a good night's sleep in the Nether?

A Because the beds explode.

Steve: I tried bringing water into the Nether.

Alex: Big mist-take.

Q Why was the zombie pigman tired?

A Because he was dead on his feet.

Q Did you hear about the snow golem that spawned in the Nether?

A It had a meltdown.

Q Why was the zombie pigman late?

A Because he was a slow pork.

GOLEM GAGS

Make snow mistake, these jokes are ironclad.

Q Why can't snow golems play football?

A Snowballs allowed.

Q What did the fire say when it met the snow golem?

A Pleased to melt you.

Q What do you call a golem that's not there?

A Snow golem.

49

PLANT PUNS AND FLOWER FUNNIES

These jokes are blooming hilarious.

Q What did the flower say when it had a little accident?

A I wet my plants!

Q Did you hear about the panda that lost its bamboo?

A It was bamboo-zled.

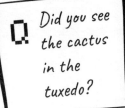 **Q** Did you see the cactus in the tuxedo?

 A It was looking sharp.

Q Which flower grows right under your nose?

 A Tulips.

 Q What do trees put on before swimming?

 A Their trunks.

WITTY WEAPONS

Let's hope you get the point with these puns.

Q What did the axe say when it was in a hurry?

A Chop chop!

Q What did Alex say when Steve held the sword upside down?

A That's not the point.

Q Why are drowned mobs great at throwing tridents?

A Because they always aim high.

Q Have you heard about the enthusiastic sword?

A It always takes a stab at everything.

Q Have you heard about the broken sword?

A It's pointless.

LOOKS LIKE BAD WITHER

Here are some more jokes, wither or not you want them!

Q Why is the wither always itchy?

A It has soul sand all over its body.

Q Why are the wither's plans so good?

A Because it can put its three heads together.

Q Why is the wither still single?

A Because it's immune to lava.

Q What do you call the wither in winter?

A A bunch of numbskulls.

Q What do you get when you cross a wither with a chicken?

A Fowl wither.

CRAFTY CHUCKLES

Let your laughter build and build.

Q Did you hear about the painter who played Minecraft?

A She was good at arts and crafts.

Q What do you call it when a witch makes something?

A Witchcraft.

Steve: My recipe book fell on my head.

Alex: That must have hurt.

Steve: Well, I've only got my shelf to blame.

Q What did one wall say to the other wall?

A Meet you at the corner.

Q Did you hear Steve had too many books?

A He never did have any shelf control.

57

SLEEP ON THESE

These jokes are simply dreamy!

Q Why can't you trust someone sleeping in a bed?

A Because they're lying.

Q Did you hear about the miner who had trouble nodding off?

A He had to rock himself to sleep.

Q Did you hear about the naughty miner who didn't want to sleep?

A He was resisting a rest.

POTION PUNS

We mixed funny bones and squid ten-tickles to brew up some giggles.

Q Why did Alex stop brewing?

A She lost her bottle.

Q What do you call a cauldron once it's warmed up?

A A hot-ron.

Q Why is brewing an enlightening experience?

A Because of all the glowstone dust.

When Alex saw Steve struggling to make a potion, she knew there was trouble brewing.

Q Did you hear about the player who threw all his potions?

A He really caused a splash.

JUST WING IT

A little bird told us you like eggs-cellent jokes.

Q What do you get when you cross a parrot with a zombie?

A A bird that talks your head off.

Q What do you get when you cross a spider with a parrot?

A A walkie-talkie.

Q How did the chicken get out of the egg?

A It hatched a plan.

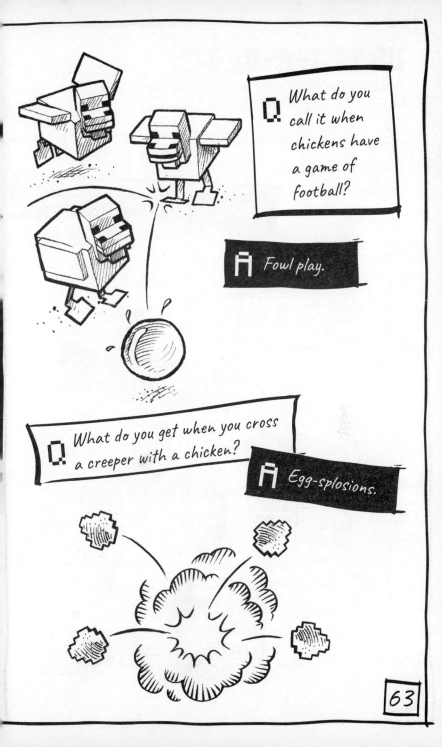

Q What do you call it when chickens have a game of football?

A Fowl play.

Q What do you get when you cross a creeper with a chicken?

A Egg-splosions.

63

CHOCK-A-BLOCK

Building rule number one: don't get stuck between a block and a hard place.

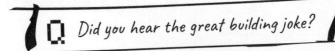

Q Did you hear the great building joke?

A Oh wait, it's not finished yet.

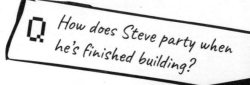

Q How does Steve party when he's finished building?

A He raises the roof.

Q What music does Steve listen to when he's building?

A Block and roll.

I'd tell you the joke about the roof, but it'd probably go over your head.

Q Did you hear about the builder who built a village on a cliff?

A He liked living on the edge.

CREEPY CRAWLIES

Hopefully these jokes won't make your skin crawl ...

Q What are spider webs good for?

A Spiders.

Q What's worse than finding a spider in your base?

A Losing a spider in your base.

Q What do you get if you cross a spider and a chicken?

A Webbed feet.

Q Why are spiders such a problem underground?

A Because they scare people out of their mines.

Q What do you get if you cross a cave spider with a cookie?

A I'm not sure, but I wouldn't try eating it.

ARACHNID ANTICS

These jokes could make you scream with laughter or terror!

Q How did Steve know the spider was angry?

A Because it was crawling up the wall.

Q Did you hear about the undercover arachnid?

A It was a spy-der.

Q Why did the spider buy a laptop?

 A Because it wanted to build a website.

 Q Why are spiders good swimmers?

 A Because they have webbed feet.

Q What do you get when you cross a creeper and a spider?

 A A creepy crawly.

TNT TITTERS

3, 2, 1 ... get ready to blow your top with giggles.

Q *Did you hear about the argument between the building and the TNT?*

A *It was blown up out of proportion.*

Q *What did Alex say when she lost her TNT?*

A *Oh, blast.*

Q What has four legs and goes 'boom'?

A Two players fighting over a block of TNT.

Q Why are explosions in the rain depressing?

A It's all boom and gloom.

Q What do you get if you cross a clock with TNT?

A A ticking time bomb.

WIT AND WIZARDRY

Combine an enchantment with this book to magic up some laughs.

Q Which flower is like an enchantment?

A A rose bush, because it has thorns.

Q Which enchantment makes fish faster?

A Ef-fish-ciency.

Q How do you start a singalong in the village?

A Just start en-chanting.

Q Which enchantment hurts flying mobs?

A Ender-smite.

Q What's a cactus's favourite enchantment?

A Sharpness.

FLUFFY FUNNIES

They might both have fluffy white coats, but mix up the polar bear and the llama at your peril!

Steve: Did you see the animal film last night?

Alex: No, what did I miss?

Steve: Just some llama drama.

Q What did the llama say when it was told to leave the village?

A Alpaca my bags.

Q What do you call a polar bear in the desert?

A Lost.

Q How do you deal with a group of hostile llamas?

A You just have to get used to spit.

Q Why are polar bears bad at conversation?

A They're afraid to break the ice.

Q What do polar bears eat for lunch?

A Icebergers.

75

WITTY WITCHES

These jokes will really make you cackle!

Q What do you call a witch covered in sand?

A A sand-witch.

Q Why did the witches stop being friends?

A They were driving each other batty.

Q What do you call a witch that won't stop scratching?

A An itch.

Q Why is it easy to confuse one witch for another?

A Because it's hard to tell which witch is which.

Q What do you call a witch in a hole?

A A ditch.

Q Why did the witch write a book?

A Because she was good at spelling.

77

FARMYARD FUNNIES

Have a giggle at these farmyard funnies.

Q Why do cows prefer the other side?

A Because the grass is always greener.

Q Did you hear about the giant cow in the tiny house?

A There wasn't mooshroom.

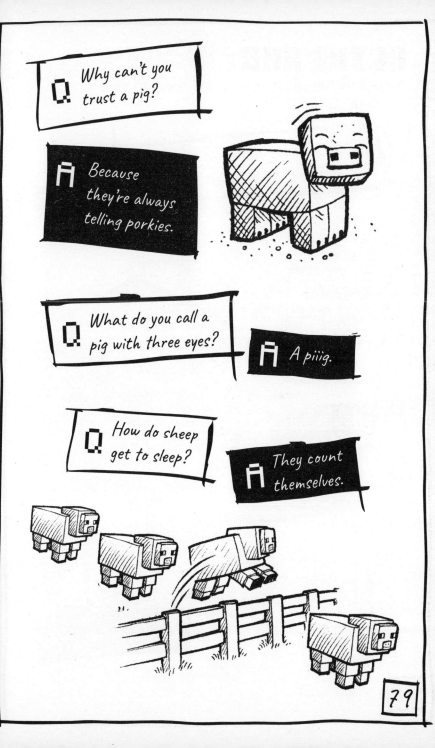

IN THE END

To get to these jokes, you'll need to find a chortle room.

Q What's the last block you should place when you finish a build?

A The End stone.

Q Why did Steve think the shulker was shy?

A Because it wouldn't come out of its shell.

Q What do you call an endermite that can't make up its mind?

A An ender-might.

Q. Why do cats like End cities?

A. Because they're made from purrpurr blocks.

Steve: I think I can hear singing ...

Alex: Must be the chorus plants.

THE END OF THE END
Stop dragon your heels and read on!

Q Why are shulkers bad at telling jokes?

A Because they always start at the End.

Q Why do shulkers hide in their shells?

A Because they're shulking.

Q How many items can you put in an empty ender chest?

A One. Aftr one, it isn't empty any more.

Q How did Steve feel when he defeated the ender dragon?

A Egg-cited.

Q What should you do when you're fed up with the End?

A You should a-void it.

83

MINE, ALL MINE!

Get back on track with this minecart full of cheer.

Q Did you hear about the player who used a potion of invisibility while riding in a minecart?

A She was trying to cover her tracks.

Q Why was the minecart so late?

A It really got off track.

Q How do you find a missing minecart?

A Just follow the tracks.

Q Why was the minecart late?

A It got sidetracked.

Steve: How many minecarts came off the rails?

Alex: I don't know, it's hard to keep track.

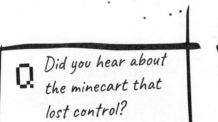

Q Did you hear about the minecart that lost control?

A It really went off the rails.

PET PUNS

Wolf down these purrfect puns.

Q What did the skeleton say to the wolf?

A Bone-appetit.

Q What do you get if you cross a wolf with a sheep?

A A wolf in sheep's clothing.

Q What do you call a messy cat?

A A shabby tabby.

Q How do you know when a cat is hurt?

A It says, 'Me-OW'.

Q What do you call a pile of kittens?

A A meowntain.

Q Why is it hard for ocelots to hide?

A Because they're always spotted.

87

HALF-BAKED HUMOUR

We hope these hot cross puns get a rise out of you.

Q What did Alex say to the tasty bread?

A I loaf you.

Q Did you hear about the villager that was stealing food?

A He was caught bread-handed.

Q When does bread rise?

A When you yeast expect it.

Q What did the angry cake say to Alex and Steve?

A You wanna piece of me?

Q Did you hear about the pumpkin pie that ran away?

A It desserted.

ENDERMANIA!
These jokes are a scream!

Q Why don't endermen like jokes about water?

A They only like dry humour.

Q Where do endermen sleep?

A Anywhere they like.

Q Why are endermen so tall?

A Because their feet smell.

Q What do you call an enderman who has lost weight?

A A slenderman.

Q Why didn't the enderman cross the road?

A Because it teleported across instead.

Q What do you call an enderman that picks up TNT?

A Extremely dangerous.

ALMOST AT THE END ... ERMAN

These jokes will teleport you to the funny dimension.

Q *What do you call a group of endermen?*

A *An enderclan.*

Q *What do you get if you cross an enderman and a village priest?*

A *An end-amen.*

Q What do you call it when Steve dresses up as an enderman?

A A pretenderman.

Q What do you call an enderman with feelings?

A A tenderman.

Q Why did the enderman live in a bungalow?

A Because it didn't like stares.

REPTILE ROARS

Read these jokes to make the ender dragon seem less scary!

Q What did the polite ender dragon say?

A Fang you very much.

Q Why is the ender dragon bad at telling stories?

A They always drag on.

Q What does the ender dragon sound like?

A Roar-some.

Q What's so special about a dragon egg?

A They're eggs-cellent, of course!

Q Which ball shouldn't you play with?

A A dragon's fireball.

Q What do you sing to the ender dragon on its birthday?

A Flappy Birthday!